CW01379307

DOGS DO SCIENCE

MATERIALS

BY ANNA CLAYBOURNE AND LUKE SÉGUIN-MAGEE

WAYLAND

First published in Great Britain in 2023 by Wayland
© Hodder and Stoughton Limited, 2023

All rights reserved.

HB ISBN: 978 1 5263 2190 9
PB ISBN: 978 1 5263 2191 6

Editor: Paul Rockett
Illustration: Luke Séguin-Magee

FSC® C104740
MIX Paper from responsible sources

Printed in China

Wayland
An imprint of Hachette Children's Group
Part of Hodder & Stoughton
Carmelite House
50 Victoria Embankment
London EC4Y 0DZ

An Hachette UK Company
www.hachette.co.uk
www.hachettechildrens.co.uk

CONTENTS

- 4 DOGS DO MATERIALS
- 6 JUMPING JACK RUSSELL
- 8 BORZOI GETS A BUMP
- 10 DOGS IN SPACE
- 12 STAFFIE'S STICK
- 14 BEAGLES AT THE BEACH
- 16 SPOT THE SPANIEL'S SINK OR SWIM
- 18 COLLIE'S COSY COAT
- 20 DALMATION IN DANGER
- 22 BACK IN TIME
- 24 WHIPPET IN WINTER
- 26 WESTIE GETS WET
- 28 PROFESSOR POOCH'S MATERIALS ROUND-UP
- 30 POODLE'S POP QUIZ
- 32 ANSWERS, FURTHER INFORMATION AND INDEX

DOGS DO MATERIALS

A PUPPY ARRIVES AT HER NEW HOME...

HERE YOU GO, PUP! YOUR NEW HOME!

OOOH! SO MUCH TO EXPLORE! SO MUCH TO CHEW!

WHAT'S THIS?

OH! IT COMES APART! FUN!

MMMM, THIS BIG SQUASHY THING IS LOVELY AND SOFT!

OOOH! FLUFFY STUFF!

OOPS! WHAT HAPPENED?

MY DRINK!

OH. THAT THING APPEARS TO HAVE BROKEN. AND NOW THERE'S WET STUFF EVERYWHERE!

SMASH!

WOW! A TOY JUST FOR ME!

FOR PUPPY X

HMMM! WHATEVER I DO TO THIS IT DOESN'T CHANGE AT ALL. I WONDER WHY?

PROFESSOR POOCH, BOFFIN BICHON, IS HERE TO ANSWER YOUR CALL!

NEWSPAPER TEARS...

IT'S ALL A MATTER OF MATERIALS!

SOFA CUSHIONS ARE FULL OF FLUFFY STUFFING...

GLASS SMASHES, AND WATER SPILLS.

WHILE A RUBBERY CHEW TOY IS TOUGH AND STRONG!

GNNNRRR! WOOF!

YOU'RE SO RIGHT, PROFESSOR! BUT WHY???

BECAUSE THEY'RE ALL MADE OF DIFFERENT MATERIALS, WHICH BEHAVE IN DIFFERENT WAYS.

THIS BOOK WILL MAKE IT ALL CRYSTAL CLEAR! READ ON!

PROF. POOCH'S BOOK OF MATERIALS FOR DOGS

JUMPING JACK RUSSELL

IN JACK RUSSELL'S HOUSE ...

THERE YOU GO KIDS -- TRY IT OUT!

WHEEE!

BOING!

INDOORS ...

WHAT'S THAT?

I WANT A GO!

OUTSIDE ...

LET ME HAVE A GO!

WOOF, WOOF!

THIS IS BRILLIANT!

I CAN JUMP SO MUCH HIGHER THAN NORMAL. IT'S LIKE MAGIC!

HOW DOES IT WORK?

BOINGGG!

LATER ...

AHA! THIS EXPLAINS IT!

THE TRAMPOLINE HAS SPRINGS AROUND THE EDGE, MADE OF BENDY METAL.

WHEN YOU LAND ON THE TRAMPOLINE, THE METAL BENDS AND THE SPRINGS STRE-E-ETCH.

UNSTRETCHED

STRETCHED

THEN THE BENDY METAL SPRINGS BACK INTO PLACE, PULLING THE TRAMPOLINE UP AGAIN -- AND YOU GO WITH IT!

IT'S GENIUS! I CAN'T WAIT FOR ANOTHER GO!

PROF. POOCH'S BOOK OF MATERIALS FOR DOGS

BUT ...

KIDS! TEATIME! BRING THE DOG IN!

AWWWWW!

LATER ...

THIS WAY!

WAHEY!

WHEEEE!

BOING!

BOING!!!

BORZOI GETS A BUMP

AT THE VET'S...

"JUST A QUICK LITTLE JAB!"

OUCH! I HATE THE VET'S!

"BYE! SEE YOU NEXT TIME!"

GET ME OUT OF HERE!

FREEDOM!

BANG! CRASH!

OOOOOOWWWWWWW! MY NOSE! WHAT HAPPENED?

"OH NO! POOR DOGGY! SHE DIDN'T REALISE THE DOOR WAS THERE!"

STUPID SEE-THROUGH DOOR! WHAT'S THAT ALL ABOUT?

"OH DEAR! IT'S CLEAR THERE'S BEEN A TRANSPARENCY ACCIDENT!

YOU SEE, THIS DOOR IS MADE OF GLASS, AND IT'S TOTALLY SEE-THROUGH -- OR, AS WE SCIENTISTS LIKE TO SAY, TRANSPARENT!"

"WHAT'S THE POINT OF THAT?"

"YES, POOCH! WHAT IS THE POINT OF THAT!? NOW I HAVE A SORE, SQUISHED NOSE!"

WELL, TRANSPARENT MATERIALS CAN BE VERY USEFUL. THE VET'S DOOR LETS IN LOTS OF LIGHT -- AND GLASS WINDOWS DO, TOO.
WE USE TRANSPARENT GLASS OR PLASTIC FOR SCREENS, MAGNIFYING GLASSES AND MY SPECS! CLEAR FOOD WRAP LETS YOU SEE WHAT'S INSIDE.
HMM, I SUPPOSE THAT IS QUITE USEFUL ...
BACK HOME ...
HA HA, LOOK AT YOU! WHAT HAPPENED?
WELL, I RAN INTO A GLASS DOOR, IF YOU MUST KNOW ...
D'OH!
RIGHT ...
HERE IT IS!
FOOD WRAP
CAT
HEY CAT! I THINK YOUR DINNER'S READY!
HEH HEH HEH!
BOING!

DOGS IN SPACE

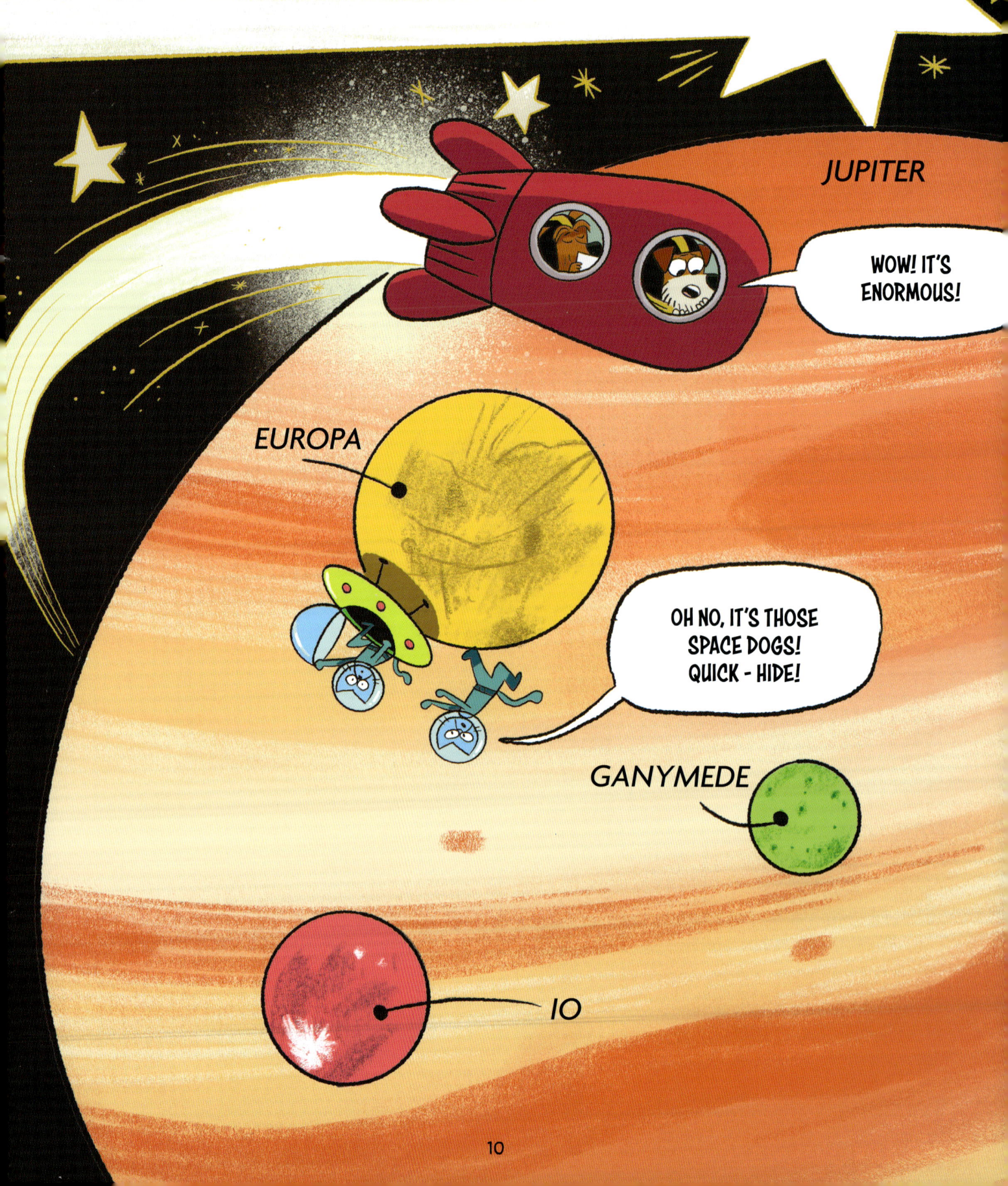

JUPITER

WOW! IT'S ENORMOUS!

EUROPA

OH NO, IT'S THOSE SPACE DOGS! QUICK - HIDE!

GANYMEDE

IO

CAPTAIN DOG'S LOG, STARDATE SATURDAY TEATIME

TODAY WE VISITED JUPITER, THE BIGGEST PLANET IN THE SOLAR SYSTEM! JUST LOOK AT IT! ORANGE, STRIPY AND COVERED IN SWIRLY STORMS -- FANTASTIC! IT'S BEEN MY LIFELONG DREAM TO COME HERE, SO NATURALLY I ASKED LIEUTENANT SCOTTIE TO SET A COURSE FOR LANDING.

CAPTAIN DOG'S LOG, STARDATE SATURDAY EVENING

IMAGINE MY DISMAY WHEN SCOTTIE SAID WE COULDN'T LAND ON JUPITER! "WE REALLY DON'T WANT TO DO THAT, CAPTAIN!" HE REPLIED. "WE'D NEVER BE SEEN AGAIN!" ACCORDING TO SCOTTIE, YOU CAN'T LAND ON JUPITER BECAUSE IT DOESN'T HAVE ANY LAND! WHAT A SPOILSPORT.

CAPTAIN DOG'S LOG, STARDATE SATURDAY NIGHT

IT TURNS OUT THAT PLANETS NEARER THE SUN, LIKE EARTH AND MARS, ARE MADE OF SOLID ROCK, AND HAVE SOLID LAND. BUT FURTHER AWAY, PLANETS LIKE JUPITER AND SATURN ARE MOSTLY MADE OF GAS AND LIQUID. IF YOU TRIED TO LAND ON THEM, YOU'D JUST SINK! THAT'S WHY THEY'RE CALLED 'GAS GIANTS'!

OTHER FINDINGS:
- SO, JUST LIKE OTHER THINGS, PLANETS ARE MADE OF DIFFERENT MATERIALS, WHICH CAN EXIST IN THREE STATES — SOLID, LIQUID AND GAS. THEY'RE CALLED THE 'STATES OF MATTER'.
- HOWEVER, THERE'S GOOD NEWS! JUPITER'S MOONS ARE SOLID, AND PERFECT FOR LANDING ON, SO WE'RE OFF FOR A PICNIC ON EUROPA INSTEAD! ACCORDING TO SCIENTISTS, IT'S ALSO A POSSIBLE HOME FOR ALIEN LIFE – EXCITING!

CALLISTO

STAFFIE'S STICK

IN THE PARK...
YAY! I LOVE THE PARK!

FETCHING THE BALL...
WOOF, WOOF!

PLAYING WITH MY STICK...
GRRRRRR!

...AND HANGING OUT WITH MY FRIENDS!
WOOF!
YAP YAP!
SNIFFETY SNIFF!

BUT THEN...
UHH!? MY STICK! MY BALL! I CAN'T SEE THEM!

THEY MUST BE LOST IN THE GRASS!

I LOVED THAT STICK! IT WAS PERFECT!

THEN...
HEY LOOK! LOADS MORE STICKS!

SO MANY TO CHOOSE FROM! I'LL TAKE THIS ONE -- LOVELY!
BUT I CAN'T FIND ANOTHER BALL! PLENTY OF STICKS, BUT NO BALLS! WHY IS THAT?
BECAUSE, MY DEAR STAFFIE, BALLS DON'T GROW ON TREES! YOU SEE, MATERIALS COME FROM DIFFERENT PLACES.
STICKS ARE MADE OF WOOD -- A NATURAL MATERIAL. THEY DO GROW ON TREES! BUT YOUR BALL WAS MADE BY HUMANS, USING PLASTIC, AN ARTIFICIAL OR HUMAN-MADE MATERIAL. TO GET ANOTHER ONE, YOU'D HAVE TO GO TO A SHOP!
I SEE ... OH WELL. I LOVED THAT BALL!
JUST THEN ...
UH, ARRRRGGHH! OOOPS!
MY BALL!!! THERE IT IS! THANK YOU, DOBERMAN!
WELL DONE, DOBERMAN! YOU HAVE YOUR USES AFTER ALL!

BEAGLES AT THE BEACH

AT THE BEACH...

SPLOSH! SPLASH!!!
WOOF, WOOF, WOOF!

WOOHOO, THIS IS FUN! CAN'T BEAT A DAY AT THE BEACH!

LATER...

PHEW, I'M WORN OUT!

AND IT'S REALLY HOT! I'M SO THIRSTY!

WELL, THERE'S PLENTY OF WATER! LET'S HAVE SOME!

SLURP!

BLEUGH! UGH! THAT'S DISGUSTING! I CAN'T DRINK THAT!

NOOOOO, YOU SILLY DOGS! DON'T DRINK THE SEAWATER!

COME ON! I'VE GOT SOME DRINKING WATER FOR YOU HERE.

SLURP! AAAAAH, THAT'S BETTER! DELICIOUS!

BUT WHAT WAS IN THE SEAWATER? WHY DID IT TASTE LIKE THAT?

YOUR HUMAN WAS RIGHT, BEAGLES! NEVER DRINK SEAWATER. YOU SEE, SEAWATER ISN'T JUST WATER -- IT'S FULL OF SALT!

AS RIVERS FLOW, THEY PICK UP SALT FROM ROCKS AND CARRY IT INTO THE SEA. THE SALT DISSOLVES IN THE WATER AND BREAKS APART INTO TINY BITS ... SO YOU CAN'T SEE IT!

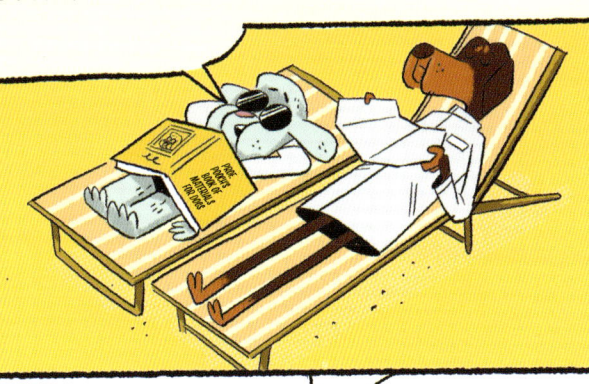

BUT YOU CAN TASTE IT! AND TOO MUCH SALT ISN'T GOOD FOR YOU.

IN FACT, MANY DIFFERENT MATERIALS CAN DISSOLVE IN WATER! ROCKS, MINERALS, SUGAR -- ALL KINDS OF THINGS!

WHAT'S WRONG, DOBERMAN?

I'M NEVER HAVING A BATH AGAIN! WHAT IF I DISSOLVE??!!

DOBERMAN MY DEAR, DO NOT PANIC! NOT EVERYTHING DISSOLVES! THESE BEAGLES WERE IN THE SEA ALL AFTERNOON AND THEY'RE PERFECTLY FINE!

PHEW!!!

SPOT THE SPANIEL'S SINK OR SWIM

WELCOME TO SPOT'S PUZZLE PAGE! IT'S TIME FOR A MIND-BENDING, MATERIAL-SORTING MYSTERY!

HERE WE HAVE A SELECTION OF LOVELY BITS AND BOBS THAT I'VE COLLECTED FROM AROUND THE HOUSE. (I DIDN'T EVEN CHEW THEM! WELL, MOST OF THEM.) THEY'RE ALL MADE OUT OF DIFFERENT MATERIALS.

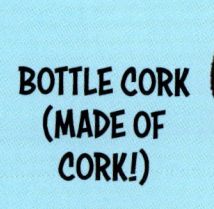

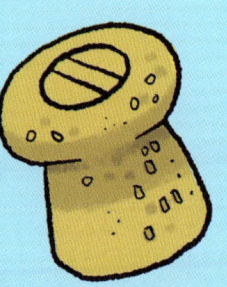

- BOTTLE CORK (MADE OF CORK!)
- WOODEN PENCIL
- PEBBLE
- METAL KEY
- COPPER COIN
- PLASTIC BUTTON
- GLASS MARBLE
- SEASHELL
- STRAWBERRY

YOUR CHALLENGE IS TO SORT THEM OUT INTO MATERIALS THAT **FLOAT** IN WATER AND MATERIALS THAT **SINK**!

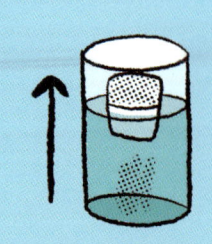

IF YOU LIKE, YOU COULD FIND OUT BY TESTING REAL-LIFE OBJECTS IN A BOWL OF WATER AT HOME (MAKE SURE YOU ASK AN ADULT TO HELP). OR JUST LOOK AT THE PICTURES AND HAVE A GUESS!

YOU SEE, SOME MATERIALS FLOAT BECAUSE THEY ARE LESS DENSE, OR HEAVY FOR THEIR SIZE, THAN WATER -- SO IT HOLDS THEM UP! THINGS THAT ARE DENSER THAN WATER SINK.

IF YOU'RE STUCK, TURN TO PAGE 32 FOR THE ANSWERS.

SPOT

PUPPY PUNS

WHERE CAN YOU FIND A SEA WITH NO WATER?

ON A MAP!

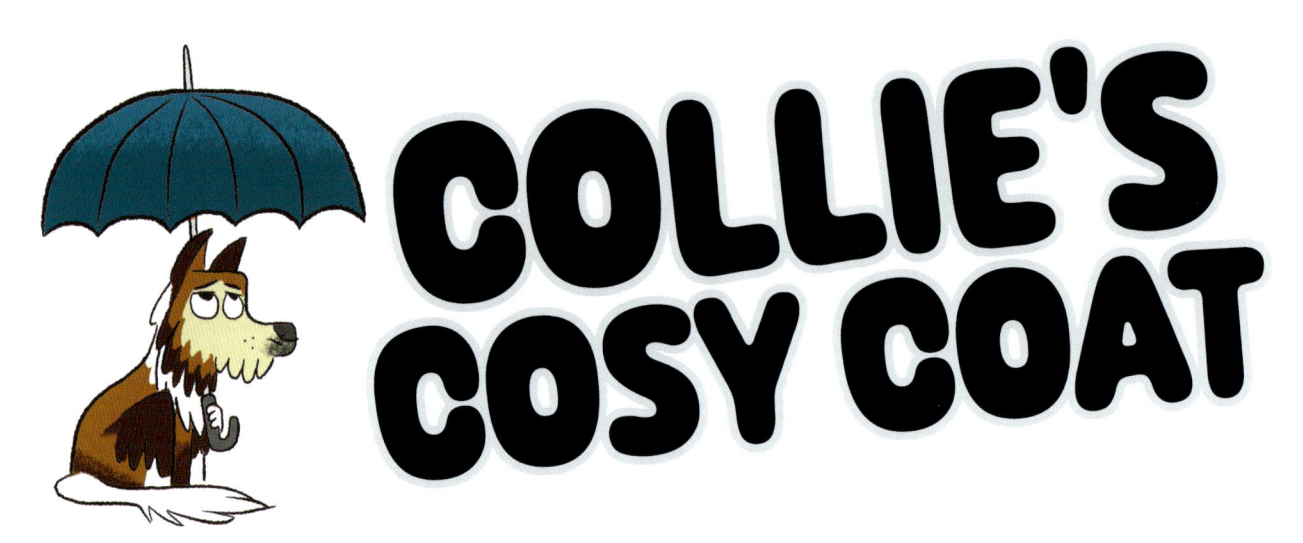

COLLIE'S COSY COAT

ON A COLD, RAINY DAY ...

OH NO ... IT DOESN'T LOOK VERY NICE OUT THERE! BUT I NEED A WALK!

COME ON, COLLIE! TIME FOR A WALK!

DON'T WORRY, YOU WON'T BE COLD! I'VE GOT YOU A NEW DOG JACKET!

OOOOH!

OOOH! STYLISH!

LET'S GO!

BUT ...

HMMM. I DON'T FEEL VERY WARM!

IN FACT, I FEEL SOAKING WET ... ... AND FREEZING! BRRRR!

OH NO, POOR COLLIE! IT'S NOT KEEPING YOU WARM AT ALL!

AHA! I SEE WHAT'S HAPPENED HERE! A MIXED-UP MATERIAL MUDDLE!

YOU SEE, THE JACKET HAS TWO LAYERS:

THIS IS A WATERPROOF MATERIAL, FOR KEEPING THE RAIN OUT ...

... AND THIS IS A THICK, FLUFFY MATERIAL THAT TRAPS HEAT, KEEPING US DOGGIES NICE AND WARM!

IT SHOULD WORK PERFECTLY -- IT'S JUST INSIDE OUT!

OOPS, IT'S INSIDE-OUT! OH DEAR! SORRY DOG!

BRRRRR! I WANT TO GO HOME!

NEXT DAY ...

OK COLLIE, YOUR JACKET IS DRY! LET'S TRY THIS AGAIN!

THIS IS GREAT! SO COSY!

HARRUMPH! WISH I HAD ONE OF THOSE!

OK CAT, YOU CAN BORROW IT -- BUT ONLY WHEN I'M NOT USING IT!

AHH, LOVELY! THIS IS THE LIFE!

DALMATIAN IN DANGER

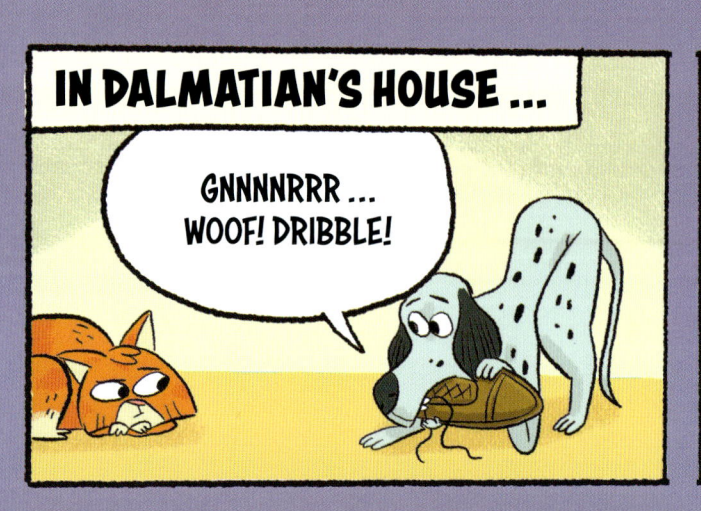

IN DALMATIAN'S HOUSE...

GNNNNRRR ... WOOF! DRIBBLE!

MUNCH! SQUISH! GRRRRR!

CHEW!!! MMMMM ... GNNNRRR ... SLURP!

OH! DON'T MIND ME -- I'M JUST HAVING A NICE TIME CHEWING THINGS! I JUST LOVE TO CHEW!

OOOH, WHAT ARE THESE!? THEY LOOK PRETTY CHEWY!

NOOOO! STOP IT DOG! DON'T CHEW THOSE!

YOU CAN'T CHEW ELECTRIC WIRES, IT'S DANGEROUS! NO CHEWING WIRES! GOOD DOG!
AWWWW! BUT WHY NOT?
LET'S SEE IF PROFESSOR POOCH'S BOOK CAN EXPLAIN THIS ...
PROF. POOCH'S BOOK OF MATERIALS FOR DOGS
METAL WIRE CARRIES ELECTRICITY
INSULATING PLASTIC COVER
I SEE! THOSE WIRES CARRY ELECTRICITY TO MAKE THINGS WORK! THE WIRE IS MADE OF METAL, A MATERIAL THAT CONDUCTS, OR CARRIES, ELECTRICITY.
IT HAS A COVER MADE OF PLASTIC, AN INSULATING MATERIAL WHICH DOESN'T CONDUCT ELECTRICITY. THAT MAKES THE WIRES SAFE TO TOUCH, AS ELECTRICITY CAN HURT YOU.
BUT IF YOU CHEW THROUGH THE COVER ...
AAARRGGHHH!
OK, I AM NEVER CHEWING ELECTRIC WIRES! SCARY! BUT WHAT ELSE CAN I CHEW?
OOOH! LOOKS CHEWY!
GRRRRRR! WOOF! DRIBBLE!
GET OFF MY BASKET, YOU SLOBBERY MUTT!

BACK IN TIME

READY FOR A JOURNEY TO THE PAST?

DR WHOODLE HERE, READY TO TRANSPORT YOU THROUGH TIME IN MY MARVELLOUS MACHINE. STEP INSIDE!

DON'T WORRY, IT WON'T TAKE LONG -- AS WE'RE ONLY GOING BACK TO 1941!

WE'RE OFF TO MEET THE IMPORTANT INVENTOR GEORGE DE MESTRAL, AND HIS EVEN MORE IMPORTANT DOG, MILKA!

DATE: 1941
THE LOCATION: SWITZERLAND

THAT'S AMAZING ... HOW DOES IT WORK!?

WHAT, THIS? OH, IT'S JUST MY RICKETY OLD TIME MACHINE ...

WOOF WOOF!

OH, HELLO ... NO, NOT THAT.

I MEAN HOW DOES THIS WORK? LOOK!

EVERY TIME WE GO FOR A WALK IN THE WOODS, WE GET COVERED IN THESE PRICKLY PLANT BURRS.

THEY STICK TO MILKA'S FUR.

BUT WHEN I PULL THEM OFF, THEY ARE ACTUALLY NOT STICKY AT ALL! IT'S VERY STRANGE!

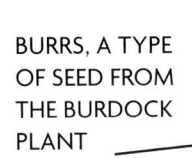

GEORGE DE MESTRAL LOOKED AT THE BURRS UNDER A MICROSCOPE AND FOUND THEIR SPIKES HAD TINY HOOKS ON THE ENDS. THEY STUCK TO FABRIC OR ANIMALS BY HOOKING ONTO TINY LOOPS OF THREAD OR FUR.

BURRS, A TYPE OF SEED FROM THE BURDOCK PLANT

DE MESTRAL REALISED HE COULD USE HOOKS AND LOOPS IN THE SAME WAY TO MAKE A STICKY MATERIAL FOR HOLDING THINGS TOGETHER. AFTER WORKING ON IT FOR SEVERAL YEARS, HE INVENTED HOOK-AND-LOOP FASTENERS, ALSO KNOWN AS VELCRO®.

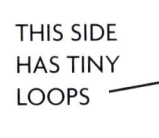

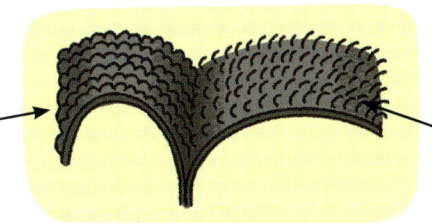

WE NOW USE IT FOR ALL KINDS OF THINGS, LIKE FASTENING TRAINERS, BAGS, COATS AND DOG JACKETS!

RRRIP!

THIS SIDE HAS TINY LOOPS

THIS SIDE HAS TINY HOOKS

EVEN ASTRONAUTS IN SPACE USE IT, TO HOLD THINGS STILL IN MICROGRAVITY.

RRRRRIP!

IT'S A GREAT EXAMPLE OF AN ARTIFICIAL MATERIAL THAT WAS INSPIRED BY PLANTS ...

AND DOG FUR! WOOF!

WHIPPET IN WINTER

ONE DAY IN WINTER ...

OOOH, WHAT'S THAT WHITE STUFF!? LOOKS LIKE FUN!!

WALKIES! COME ON!

COME OUTSIDE AND SEE THE SNOW!

OUTSIDE ...

THIS SNOW STUFF IS GREAT! IT'S ALL FLUFFY AND SOFT, AND YOU CAN MAKE BALLS OUT OF IT!

BUT IT'S ALSO COLD. VERY COLD!

HEY, PUDDLES! MY FAVOURITE! TIME FOR A NICE SPLASH!

BUT ...

HUH? IT'S ALL HARD! WHAT HAPPENED?

I LIKE THIS SNOWBALL SO MUCH, I'M GOING TO KEEP IT!
BUT ...
AWWW? NOW MY SNOWBALL HAS TURNED INTO WATER!
THIS IS ALL VERY CONFUSING. I NEED TO FIND OUT WHAT'S GOING ON!
HMMM ... HERE WE ARE. IT SEEMS MATERIALS CAN CHANGE BETWEEN LIQUID AND SOLID ... AND IT DEPENDS HOW HOT OR COLD THEY ARE!
PROF. POOCH'S BOOK OF MATERIALS FOR DOGS
WHEN WATER GETS REALLY COLD, IT FREEZES INTO SOLID SNOW OR ICE. WHEN IT WARMS UP, IT MELTS AND TURNS INTO LIQUID WATER AGAIN! IT'S CALLED CHANGING STATE!
20°C = COSY INDOOR TEMPERATURE
0°C = FREEZING TEMPERATURE
IN ICE, THE MOLECULES (TINY PARTS) IN THE WATER ARE FIXED TOGETHER
IN WATER, THE MOLECULES IN THE WATER MOVE AROUND FREELY
IT ALL MAKES SENSE NOW. BUT I STILL WISH I COULD KEEP A SNOWBALL!
HEY! I KNOW! FETCH ANOTHER SNOWBALL ...
... AND PUT IT IN HERE! RIGHT THERE, NEXT TO THE PEAS.
GENIUS! THANKS CAT!

WESTIE GETS WET

IN WESTIE'S HOUSE ...

MMMM, SQUIRRELS!

SNORE!

JUST THEN ...

OOPS! CLUMSY!

ARRGH! URGH, I'M SOAKING! WOOF! STUPID CAT!

HEH HEH!

BRRRR, I'M ALL COLD AND WET NOW! I NEED TO WARM UP!

DRIP ... DRIP ... DRIP ...

OOH, THERE'S A NICE HOT HEATER.

AAAAH, LOVELY AND WARM!

HALF AN HOUR LATER ...

OOOH, THAT'S BETTER. I'VE WARMED UP NOW. I'M COMPLETELY DRY TOO! ALL THE WATER'S GONE! HOW DID THAT HAPPEN?

WELL, WESTIE, THE WATER DOES STILL EXIST. IT'S JUST NOT ON YOU ANY MORE!

UH? THEN WHERE IS IT?

IN THE AIR!

LIQUID WATER IS MADE OF TINY MOLECULES THAT ARE MOVING AROUND. AT THE SURFACE, MOLECULES SLOWLY ESCAPE INTO THE AIR, AND BECOME A GAS, OR EVAPORATE, AS WE SCIENTISTS SAY!

THE WARMER IT IS, THE FASTER THE MOLECULES MOVE AND THE FASTER THEY EVAPORATE! THAT'S WHY YOU'RE ALREADY DRY!

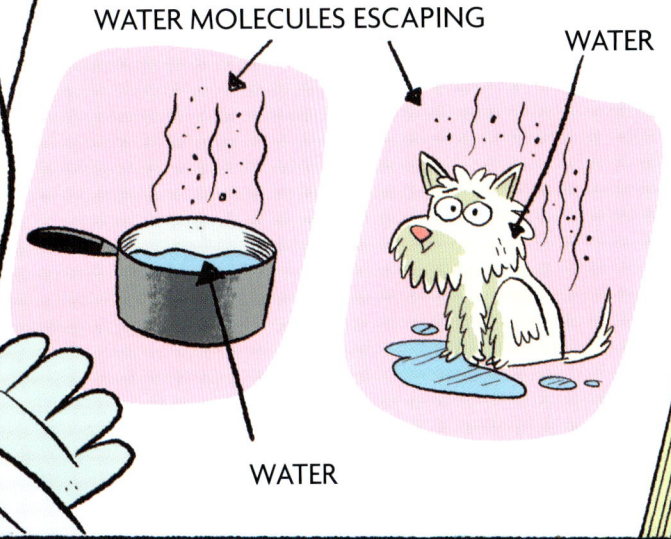

WATER MOLECULES ESCAPING

WATER

WATER

THIS IS ALSO WHY WASHING DRIES FASTER IN WARM SUNSHINE!

BRILLIANT! RIGHT, TIME TO GET MY REVENGE...

PERFECT!

HEH HEH!

MREEEOWWW!

PROFESSOR POOCH'S MATERIALS ROUND-UP

"THERE WE ARE, DOBERMAN! YOU'RE NOW AN EXPERT ON THE SCIENCE OF MATERIALS!"

"UM ... AM I?"

"WELL, ALMOST! ALL YOU NEED IS A LITTLE REMINDER OF ALL THE TOPICS IN THE BOOK. ARE YOU READY?"

"ER ..."

"LET'S GO!"

WHAT ARE MATERIALS?
Materials are simply all the different kinds of stuff that things are made of – like wood, glass, water, rubber, paper, plastic, metal and so on.

As puppy discovered, materials can do different things and behave in different ways.

BENDY AND STRETCHY MATERIALS
Some materials can bend or stretch, then spring back to how they were before. The metal springs on Jack Russell's trampoline, for example!

SEE-THROUGH MATERIALS
Glass, water, and some kinds of plastic are see-through, or transparent. That can sometimes make them hard to see – as poor old Borzoi discovered ...

STATES OF MATTER
You'll usually find materials in one of three forms – solid, liquid or gas. They're called the states of matter. As Captain Dog discovered, the planet Jupiter is made of gas, so you can't land on it.

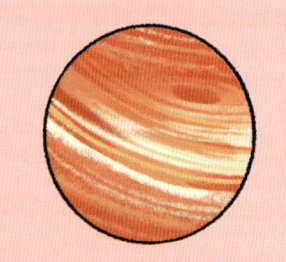

NATURAL AND ARTIFICIAL
Materials come from the world around us. But some are in their natural state, and others are artificial, or human-made, by making changes to natural materials.

Staffie's stick is made of wood, a natural material, but his ball is made from plastic, an artificial material. Humans make plastic using oil from underground.

DISSOLVING
Some materials can dissolve in a liquid, like when salt dissolves in water. The salt breaks apart into tiny bits that are too small to see. However, the beagles could taste the salt dissolved in the seawater when they tried to drink it!

FLOATING
Materials also have different densities – that means how heavy something is compared to its size. If a material is less dense than water, it will float in water. And if it's denser than water, it will sink!

WARM AND WATERPROOF
Humans use different kinds of materials for making clothes – including jackets for dogs! Soft, fluffy materials trap warm air and keep us cosy. Waterproof materials keep the rain out. Collie's jacket has both – but it only works if the waterproof layer is on the outside!

CONDUCTING ELECTRICITY
Electrical wires have to be made from special materials! A conducting material, such as copper or another metal, conducts or carries the electricity. It must be covered with an insulating material, such as plastic, that doesn't conduct electricity, to keep it safe.
And you must **never** chew through it!

INVENTING NEW MATERIALS
Those clever old humans have invented lots of new materials over the years, including plastics, steel (a mixture of iron and other ingredients), and handy hook-and-loop fasteners! The fasteners were inspired by the tiny hooks on plant burrs, that cling to animal fur.

> SORRY PROFESSOR, WHAT WERE YOU JUST SAYING? I WAS THINKING ABOUT SQUIRRELS ...

CHANGING STATE
Materials can exist in the three states of matter, solid, liquid or gas. And they can also change their state. For example, water can freeze into ice when it gets cold enough ... then melt again when it warms up. And liquid water can also evaporate into a gas in the air.

POODLE'S POP QUIZ

POODLE HERE, WITH A PERPLEXING POP QUIZ TO BOGGLE YOUR BRAIN!

THINK YOU KNOW ALL ABOUT MATERIALS? LET'S FIND OUT! HEH HEH HEH!

SOME OF THE ANSWERS CAN BE FOUND IN THE PAGES OF THIS BOOK. FOR OTHERS, YOU MIGHT HAVE TO DO A LITTLE RESEARCH!

1. Why do trampolines make dogs bounce?
A. Because dogs are naturally bouncy.
B. Because trampolines are full of air.
C. Because of the stretchy springs.

2. What's another word for see-through?
A. Transparent
B. Transport
C. Tragopan

3. What kind of planet is Jupiter?
A. A gas guzzler
B. A gas giant
C. A gas goblin

4. Which of these is NOT a natural material?
A. Seashell
B. Nylon
C. Cotton

5. Which of these things does seawater contain?
A. Salt
B. Gold
C. Fish

6. Most kinds of rock sink in water, but which kind floats?
A. Marble
B. Slate
C. Pumice

7. Which of these materials would make the cosiest dog blanket?
A. Paper
B. Clear food wrap
C. Wool

8. What was the name of inventor George de Mestral's dog?
A. Milka
B. Minion
C. Millicent

9. When water freezes into ice, it's called ...?
A. A change of scene
B. A change of trousers
C. A change of state

10. Where's the best place to dry your washing?
A. In the sunshine
B. In the cellar
C. In the sink

Turn to page 32 for the answers!

PUPPY PUNS

HOW DO YOU KNOW IF YOUR DOG IS A BIT SLOW?

IT CHASES PARKED CARS!

ANSWERS

SPOT THE SPANIEL'S SINK OR SWIM

Did you work out which materials would sink or swim?

SINK:  Copper coin,  Metal key,  Plastic button,  Seashell,  Pebble,  Glass marble

SWIM: Bottle cork,  Wooden pencil,  Strawberry

POODLE'S POP QUIZ

1. C
2. A
3. B
4. B
5. All of them! Trick question!
6. C
7. C
8. A
9. C
10. A

FURTHER INFORMATION

OTHER BOOKS ON MATERIALS

A Question of Science: Why is Ice Slippery? by Anna Claybourne (2021) Wayland

Be a Scientist: Investigating Materials by Jacqui Bailey (2019) Wayland

Discover and Do!: Materials by Jane Lacey (2021) Franklin Watts

INDEX

burrs 23, 29

electric wires 21, 29
evaporation 27, 29

Jupiter 10–11, 28

materials
   artificial 13, 23, 28–29
   bendy 7, 28

materials *(continued)*
   conducting 21, 29
   dissolving 15, 29
   floating 16–17, 29
   natural 13, 28
   see-through 8–9, 28
   sinking 16–17, 29
   stretchy 7, 28
   transparent 8–9, 28
   warm 19, 29

materials *(continued)*
   waterproof 19, 29
Mestral, George de 22–23

states of matter 11, 25–29

velcro 23, 29

water 24–27